EVERYDAY STEM

HOW WI-FI WORKS

A. S. GINTZLER

Cavendish Square
New York

Published in 2019 by Cavendish Square Publishing, LLC
243 5th Avenue, Suite 136, New York, NY 10016

First Edition

Website: cavendishsq.com

Library of Congress Cataloging-in-Publication Data

Names: Gintzler, A. S., author.
Title: How Wi-Fi works / A.S. Gintzler.
Description: New York : Cavendish Square, 2019. | Series: Everyday STEM |
Includes bibliographical references and index. |
Identifiers: LCCN 2017052591 (print) | LCCN 2017058766 (ebook) |
ISBN 9781502637635 (ebook) | ISBN 9781502637604 (library bound) |
ISBN 9781502637611 (pbk.) | ISBN 9781502637628 (6 pack)
Subjects: LCSH: IEEE 802.11 (Standard)--Juvenile literature. | Wireless LANS--Juvenile literature.
Classification: LCC TK5105.5668 (ebook) | LCC TK5105.5668 .G565 2019 (print) | DDC 004.6/8--dc23
LC record available at https://lccn.loc.gov/2017052591

Editorial Director: David McNamara
Editor: Meghan Lamb
Copy Editor: Nathan Heidelberger
Associate Art Director: Amy Greenan
Designer: Christina Shults
Production Coordinator: Karol Szymczuk
Photo Research: J8 Media

The photographs in this book are used by permission and through the courtesy of:
Cover, p. 1 Ijansempoi/Shutterstock.com; p. 4 Wavebreakmedia/iStock/Thinkstock.com; p. 6 Prasit photo/Moment/Getty Images; p. 7 Romrodphoto/Shutterstock.com; p. 8 ColorBlind Images/The Image Bank/Getty Images; p. 9, 21 Monkey Business Images/Shutterstock.com; p. 10 Mellimage/Shutterstock.com; p. 11 MEHAU KULYK/SCIENCE PHOTO LIBRARY/Getty Images; p. 12 DGLimages/Shutterstock.com; p. 15 Bruno Muff/Photodisc/Getty Images; p. 16 Vasin Lee/Shutterstock.com; p. 18 Maksim Shmeljov/Shutterstock.com; p. 22 Roman Samborskyi/Shutterstock.com; p. 23 Casezy idea/Shutterstock.com.

Printed in the United States of America

CONTENTS

Wi-Fi lets you use computers and devices almost anywhere without wires.

CHAPTER 1

WHAT IS WI-FI?

Wi-Fi is a way to connect to the **internet**. It works without using wires. Wi-Fi carries information to our computers, video game systems, and other devices. It carries information on invisible **airwaves**. Wi-Fi makes it easier to use your computer. It also makes it easy to use your gaming system.

Going Wireless

With Wi-Fi, you don't need a wire connection. Wi-Fi gives us freedom to move our devices around the house. You always get a **signal**. The signal comes on airwaves. Airwaves travel at the speed of light.

The symbol for Wi-Fi shows lines curved like airwaves.

Before Wi-Fi, every device needed its own wire connection. This was a problem because people moved laptops around a lot. They

With Wi-Fi, you can play video games in any room at home.

needed the freedom to go online without wires. Wi-Fi technology is wireless. It doesn't use wires.

Wi-Fi makes it simple to go online. Now, we can send messages from almost anywhere. All we need is Wi-Fi to connect us. It gets us online without wires.

We use Wi-Fi at airports and other public places.

Wi-Fi is also used outside our homes. We use it in stores, libraries, and other places. People use it at work. Wi-Fi gives us mobility. Mobility is freedom to move around.

Imagine all the people at airports with laptops. They all want to go online. But there aren't enough wire connections. Instead, Wi-Fi uses airwaves. People can go online without

WHO INVENTED WI-FI?

Scientists worked together in teams to invent Wi-Fi.

Wi-Fi wasn't invented by just one person. Wi-Fi was invented by teams of scientists and engineers. A team in Australia invented the first wireless **network**. The team was led by John O'Sullivan. He worked on ways to make radio waves carry information.

Another team in Holland made networks work better. The team was led by an engineer named Vic Hayes. He helped create the first network called Wi-Fi.

wires. We can take our laptops and tablets with us. Wi-Fi keeps us connected. We can get the information we need wherever we go.

Waves and Networks

Airwaves are also called radio waves. Radio waves are like ripples on a pond. Have you ever thrown a rock into a lake? Did you see the circles ripple out? One circle follows another. The distance between one circle and the next is called the wavelength. The number of circles that pass by in one

Wi-Fi travels on radio waves that move like ripples on water.

second is called the **frequency**. The more circles that go by each second, the higher the frequency.

Radio waves spread in the same way as ripples. But you can't see radio waves. They travel through the air,

Radio waves travel through the air, but they are invisible.

FAST FACT

Youth HotSpot is an app in Germany. It helps people find Wi-Fi **hot spots**. The app connects to an online map. It shows the best Wi-Fi hot spots in each city.

We use Wi-Fi networks in our classrooms at school.

but they are invisible. Radio waves make Wi-Fi work without wires.

Radios and some TVs use radio waves. Cell phones also use radio waves. Radio waves can have different frequencies. Some have high frequencies, or more wave peaks per second. Others have low frequencies, or fewer peaks. High-frequency radio waves carry more information. Low-frequency waves carry less.

Computers send and receive a lot of information. They need radio waves with very high frequencies

To use Wi-Fi, you need a network. A network is a group of computers or other devices. They connect to the internet together. It's like a group of friends talking to each other.

FAST FACT

Where is the biggest Wi-Fi hot spot in the world? It's at a college in Holland. The hot spot has 650 connections. It's one giant hot spot. It covers 350 acres (142 hectares).

CAN WI-FI BE BETTER?

Wi-Fi has changed our lives. It lets us connect to the internet without wires. Wi-Fi makes using computers a lot easier. We now have the freedom to move our computers around our homes. We don't need separate **cable** connections. One connection brings the internet indoors. It reaches our computers and devices using Wi-Fi.

Wi-Fi creates networks we can use in public spaces. Wireless hot spots are almost everywhere. In some places, there are even Wi-Fi hot spots outdoors. Wi-Fi signals can travel up to 150 feet (46 meters) indoors. They can travel up to 300 feet (92 m) outdoors. But is that far enough?

Mobile phones can reach signals up to 45 miles (72 kilometers) away. That's so much farther than Wi-Fi!

CAN WI-FI BE BETTER?

Someday we'll use Wi-Fi signals even on mountaintops!

Can scientists make Wi-Fi reach longer distances? That's the challenge. Imagine using your gaming system anywhere. In the future, Wi-Fi will travel much farther. It will make our lives even easier.

People use Wi-Fi networks in public spaces called hubs or hot spots.

Wi-Fi uses wireless networks. You probably have a Wi-Fi network in your home. It lets you move from room to room with a laptop. Every computer, tablet, or game system in your home is part of the network.

Wi-Fi networks in public places are called hubs. They are also called hot spots. Your local library or sandwich shop is probably a hot spot. Many train stations and bus stations are hot spots. Some schools have Wi-Fi networks in classrooms. Your school could be a Wi-Fi hub. With Wi-Fi, students can go online at their desks. They connect without wires. Information travels to them on radio waves. Computers send and receive a lot of information. They need radio waves with very high frequencies.

Wi-Fi helps us send messages between devices without wires.

CHAPTER 2

HOW DOES WI-FI WORK?

Wi-Fi uses radio waves that travel through the air. But radio waves need a kick to get where they need to go. They are like a soccer ball. The ball doesn't move until you kick it.

Radio waves get their kick from **electricity**. Electricity is energy that travels through wires. Wi-Fi starts with electricity. An electric wire brings the internet inside your home. Then, the electric signal gets changed to Wi-Fi.

Wi-Fi Routers

The change happens inside a device called a **router**. A router is a small box with different parts inside. One part is called a **modem**. The modem connects to a special cable. It brings the internet to the router. Then, the router gives the electricity a kick.

The router sends the kick out in waves. It changes electric signals into radio waves. The invisible waves travel through your home. This makes a Wi-Fi network within your home.

Wi-Fi waves need an electric "kick" to get started, like a soccer ball.

But how does Wi-Fi reach your computer or gaming system?

Picture the soccer ball. It gets kicked down a field. The ball is kicked from one player to another. Wi-Fi moves on radio waves. The waves

THE WIRELESS SOLUTION

Wi-Fi is wireless, so we can go online anywhere and anytime.

Wi-Fi solved an important problem. Before Wi-Fi, every computer needed its own wire connection. Every device used a cable to go online. But people needed to move their laptops around. Wires and cables made it hard. Wi-Fi changed all that. Instead of wires, Wi-Fi uses radio waves. Radio waves travel through the air without wires. They are invisible. That's why Wi-Fi is called "wireless." Wi-Fi makes it easy to go online from almost anywhere.

A router is a small box with one or more antennae. It changes electric signals into Wi-Fi.

move like a soccer ball. The router is like the player who kicks the ball. The router gets Wi-Fi moving. But something else helps the router give the ball a kick.

Take a look at a router. You'll see that it has a small **antenna**. The antenna receives an electric signal. The signal comes from the internet. The antenna sends the signal to your computer on radio waves. The antenna puts the waves in motion. It's like the foot that kicks the ball. Radio waves travel to your laptop or gaming system. Your device receives the information. Then it changes it back to an electric signal.

When you kick a ball, it moves quickly. It also shakes and vibrates. The same thing happens to an electric signal. The router makes electricity shake and vibrate. This makes radio waves. They

FAST FACT

Imagine calling Wi-Fi by another name. When Wi-Fi was invented, people didn't know what to call it. They thought of DragonFly, FlankSpeed and WaveLAN. But Wi-Fi won.

shake like a kicked ball. Then, they go to all the devices in your Wi-Fi network.

When you send an email from your computer, it needs to go to the internet. It's like kicking the ball back. Your computer changes the email to an electric signal, then back to radio waves. The waves travel back to the router. The router changes the waves back to electricity. Then, your message goes out to the internet.

Wi-Fi Rides the Wave

Wi-Fi wasn't invented overnight. It was a process of trial and error. Scientists and engineers did many experiments with electricity and radio waves.

When electricity moves in a wire, it creates waves. Those waves shake and move away from the wire. They move like ripples on a lake. Scientists have studied these waves for a long time. They first discovered radio waves in the 1880s. That's more than one hundred years ago. They used them to carry radio signals. Later, they used them to carry TV signals.

Scientists learned that high-frequency radio waves carry more information. They had to

FAST FACT

Around the world, about 9 billion devices use Wi-Fi at home. But there are only 7.6 billion people. So there are 1.4 billion more devices in homes than people.

find just the right frequency for Wi-Fi. They experimented with many different frequencies. They found that Wi-Fi needs a blend of frequencies, some high and others higher. They learned how to vary the frequency. This blend became the Wi-Fi signal.

Wi-Fi signals create networks. A network connects devices to the internet. Wi-Fi creates networks without wires. They are called wireless networks. Wi-Fi changed how people use computers. People can now use computers without cables. We use wireless networks at home and at work. We use them for our laptops, tablets, and video games. Wi-Fi keeps us connected.

TECHNOLOGY TIMELINE

1880s Heinrich Hertz proves the existence of radio waves.

1906 Reginald Fessenden becomes the first person to transmit his voice wirelessly, using radio waves.

1996 John O'Sullivan and his team create the first wireless network.

1997 Vic Hayes and his team create the first wireless network called Wi-Fi.

2017 Wi-Fi speed is doubled with new Wave 2 speed.

GLOSSARY

airwaves Invisible waves that carry information through the air. Also called radio waves.

antenna The part of a router that sends a signal to computers using radio waves.

cable A thick wire that carries electricity.

electricity Energy carried through wires.

frequency The number of peaks of a wave per second.

hot spot A wireless (Wi-Fi) network. Also called a hub.

internet The worldwide computer network.

modem A box that brings internet signals indoors.

network A group of devices connected to the internet.

router A box that changes electric signals into radio waves.

signal Information carried by electricity or radio waves.

FIND OUT MORE

BOOKS

McLean, Lyn. *Wireless Wise Kids: Safer Ways to Use Mobile and Wireless Technology.* Sylvania, Australia: Envirobook, 2012.

Windsor, Diane. *How Do Computers Talk to Each Other?* Allen, TX: Techni-Kids Book Series, 2013.

WEBSITES

Ask Dr. Universe

https://askdruniverse.wsu.edu/ask

PBS Kids: Wi-Fi Balloons

http://pbskids.org/designsquad/blog/wi-fi-balloons

INDEX

Page numbers in **boldface** are illustrations.

ABOUT THE AUTHOR

A. S. Gintzler authored the six-book *Rough and Ready* historical series for John Muir Publications, coauthored the award-winning *Bizarre & Beautiful* nature series, and edited *My Family, The Jacksons* for the Writers' Voices Literacy Project. He is an editor and reporter for Scholastic and other educational publishers, including Macmillan, McGraw-Hill, and SRA.